THE SECOND AMENDMENT is under siege, and not for the first time. Today's war on Second Amendment rights, led by President Obama and New York City Mayor Michael Bloomberg, continues an American culture war that has been going on for half a century. The roots of the gun-control movement can be traced back even further, to Reconstruction and attempts to disarm the freedmen, and before that to the British gun-confiscation program that sparked the American Revolution.

President Obama, having finished his last election, is wielding his newfound flexibility and using the murders at Sandy Hook Elementary School in Newtown, Conn., to promote massive bans on firearms and magazines. Yet the president's prohibitions would have made no difference at Sandy Hook. The killer fired 150 rounds during the 20 minutes it took the police to arrive — a rate of fire that could be duplicated by any firearm produced in the past 150 years. He changed magazines repeatedly, dumping half-full magazines on the floor.

The gun-coits micro-issues du jour – plastic guns, "cop-killer bullets," so-called assault weapons, waiting periods, gun registration, and so on. The first three things on the list do not really exist. All the issues are simply the battles of the day in a much larger struggle. What is ultimately at stake is the same question that precipitated the American Revolution: whether the American people are the sovereigns in their own country or whether they should be ruled from above, for their own good, according to the supposedly benevolent commands of the elitist rulers of a top-down, European-style society.

The History of the Right to Keep and Bear Arms

Self-defense is the most fundamental of all natural rights. So agreed the founders of international law, including Francisco de Vitoria, Francisco Suárez, Hugo Grotius, Samuel Pufendorf, and Emmerich de Vattel. They built the classical system of international law through moral and logical reasoning, starting with self-evident truths about individual human rights. Foremost among these rights was self-defense.

A necessary corollary to the natural right of self-defense is the right to defensive arms.

What is ultimately at stake is the same question that precipitated the American Revolution: whether the American people are the sovereigns in their own country or whether they should be ruled from above.

For most people, some sort of arm is the only practical way in which they can vindicate their inherent right of self-defense. A woman who is attacked by a gang of three rapists usually needs a weapon to defend herself.

Thus, as the U.S. Supreme Court correctly stated in the 1876 case *U.S. v. Cruikshank*, the Second Amendment right to bear arms, like the First Amendment right to assemble, is an inherent human right that predates the Constitution. The First and Second Amendments protect these rights but do not create them. Rather, each right "is found wherever civilization exists."

Or, as John Locke wrote in *The Second Treatise of Civil Government*, because God has created every person, every person therefore has the right and the duty to protect his or her God-given life from criminals, including criminal governments.

John Adams and Thomas Jefferson disagreed on much. But they agreed on the fundamental right to self-defense. Adams supported "arms in the hands of citizens, to be used at individual discretion" for "private self-defence." Like Adams, Jefferson was a great admirer of the Italian scholar Cesare Beccaria, who founded the modern science of criminology, with his international best seller *On Crimes* and *Punishments* (*Dei Delitti e Delle Pene*). An oft-quoted passage from Beccaria observes:

> *The laws which forbid men to bear arms . . . only disarm those who are neither inclined nor determined to commit crimes. Can it be supposed that those who have the courage to violate the most sacred laws of humanity and the most important in the civil code will respect the lesser and more arbitrary laws . . . ? These laws make the victims of attack worse off and improve the position of the assailant. They do not reduce the murder rate but increase it, because an unarmed man can be attacked with more confidence than an armed man.*

The Colonies, the Revolution, and the Constitution

To the Americans of the 13 colonies, self-defense was both a right and a duty. Americans had been used to having firearms from the first days of European settlement. Unlike in Europe – where the aristocracy maintained a monopoly on hunting – hunting in America was wide open from the first days of white settlement (indeed, from the days when the first Indians crossed the Bering Strait).

All colonies except Pennsylvania required gun ownership by militiamen (most adult males). Many colonies also mandated gun ownership by the head of a household – including a woman, if she was the head – and sometimes required the carrying of guns when traveling or when going to public meetings, such as church services.

The right and duty of self-defense applied to a householder protecting her children and to militiamen protecting their communities from foreign enemies or from tyranny. Self-defense was a seamless web; the difference between self-defense against a criminal invader in the home, against a gang of highway robbers, or against a criminal tyrant with his standing army was only one of scale. The tyrant's gang was just bigger than the other ones.

The American Revolution began because of gun control. For years the Americans and the British intensely disputed whether the king and Parliament had the authority to govern the domestic affairs of the Americans and tax their internal trade. The dispute turned into a war when King George and his ministers attempted to disarm the Americans.

In the fall of 1774, the king embargoed the delivery of firearms and gunpowder to America. At the same time, royal governors began sending out the Redcoats to seize the "public arms" – the firearms and ammunition that some colonies stored in central armories to supply arms to militiamen who could not afford their own. The reason these seizures did not start an immediate war was that they were carried

---

The right and duty of self-defense applied to a householder protecting her children and to militiamen protecting their communities from foreign enemies or from tyranny.

---

out in predawn raids, before any resistance could assemble.

But in the early hours of April 19, 1775, Paul Revere and William Dawes rode to warn the people that the British were coming. The spark struck out by their steeds in their flight kindled the land into flame.

Church bells rang and guns fired, spreading alarm. The Americans turned back the British at Concord Bridge. Although the British accomplished their objective to seize guns during house-to-house searches at Lexington and Concord, the Americans swarmed into action, harrying the British on their retreat back to Boston. "Every man was his own commander," one American later recalled. The British suffered far more casualties than the Americans that day and might have been wiped out, had not the Americans begun to run out of gunpowder.

The British gun-confiscation campaign continued, with the British navy burning down Falmouth (today known as Portland, Maine) when the citizens refused to surrender their arms.

During the war, the American militia usually needed support from the Continental Army to prevail in open-field battles against British regulars. But everywhere, the militia, on their own, denied the British access to the countryside. Although the British, with control of the sea, could move quickly from one seaport to another, wherever they went there would be instant armed resistance, for the militia would rise wherever the British deployed. As historian Daniel Boorstin later put it, "The American center was everywhere and nowhere – in each man himself."

Recognizing that an armed people could not be governed without consent, the British proposed (as detailed in British Under Secretary of State William Knox's "What Is Fit to Be Done with America?") that once the Americans had been defeated, "the Arms of all the People should be taken away." American manufacture of firearms would be outlawed and the militias prohibited. Firearms were not only a tool that the Americans used to fight for self-government, but firearms possession in itself also fostered the spirit of self-government.

The original public meaning of the Second Amendment, and its analogues in state constitutions, was safeguarding the natural right to own and carry arms for all legitimate purposes. This included the inherent natural right of self-defense (which was not controversial at the time), and it also ensured that

---

Before the Civil War, the great antislavery writer Lysander Spooner used the Second Amendment to argue that slavery was unconstitutional.

---

there would be an armed body of people from whom the militia could be drawn. As Michigan Supreme Court Justice Thomas Cooley, the most eminent constitutional scholar of the latter 19th century, wrote, "The meaning of the provision undoubtedly is, that the people, from whom the militia must be taken, shall have the right to keep and bear arms; and they need no permission or regulation of law for the purpose."

The Racist Origins of Gun Control

Before the Civil War, the great antislavery writer Lysander Spooner used the Second Amendment to argue that slavery was unconstitutional. Since a slave is a person who cannot possess arms, and the Second Amendment guarantees that all persons can possess arms, no person in the United States, therefore, can be a slave. "The right of a man 'to keep and bear arms,' is a right palpably inconsistent with the idea of his being a slave," Spooner wrote.

On the other hand, in the infamous *Dred Scott* decision, U.S. Supreme Court Chief Justice Roger B. Taney announced that free blacks were not U.S. citizens; if they were, he warned, free blacks would have the right "to keep and carry arms wherever they went."

Immediately after the Civil War, Southern states enacted Black Codes that were designed to keep the ex-slaves in de facto slavery and submission. Mississippi's provision was typical: no freedman "shall keep or carry firearms of any kind, or any ammunition" without police permission. In areas where the Ku Klux Klan took control, "almost universally the first thing done was to disarm the negroes and leave them defenseless," recounted the civil-rights attorney Albion Tourgée, who represented Homer Plessy in *Plessy v. Ferguson*. The Ku Klux Klan was America's first gun-control group, as well as America's first domestic terrorist organization.

Congress responded with the Freedmen's Bureau Act, insisting that "the constitutional right to bear arms, shall be secured to and enjoyed by all the citizens." Congress followed up with the Civil Rights Act and the 14th Amendment to ensure that no state could ever again violate the civil rights of Americans.

Repeatedly, the congressional proponents of the 14th Amendment announced that one of its key purposes was to guarantee that the freedmen could exercise their Second Amendment right to own guns for self-defense, especially against Klansmen. Senator Samuel Pomeroy (R-Kan.) extolled the three "indispensable" "safeguards of liberty under our form of government": the sanctity of the home, the right to vote, and "the right to bear arms ... [so] if the cabin door of the freedman is broken open and the intruder enters ... then should a well-loaded musket be in the hand of the occupant to send the polluted wretch to another world."

Reconstruction and the 14th Amendment forced Southern states to repeal laws explicitly forbidding blacks to have guns. So the white-supremacist legislature in Tennessee enacted the 1871 "Army and Navy" law, barring the sale of any handguns except the "Army and Navy model." The ex-Confederate soldiers already had their high-quality Army and Navy guns. But cash-poor freedmen could barely afford lower-cost, simpler firearms not of the Army and Navy quality.

Many Southern states followed Tennessee's lead, with facially neutral laws banning inexpensive guns or requiring permits to own or carry a gun. As one Florida judge explained, the laws were "passed for the purpose of disarming the negro laborers ... [and] never intended to be applied to the white population." (*Watson v. Stone*, Florida, 1941.)

Jim Crow laws became the foundation of gun control in America. These laws spread north in the early decades of the 20th century, aimed primarily at immigrants (Italians and Jews in New York City) or labor agitators (California), or in response to blacks' having defended themselves against race riots (Missouri and Michigan).

In the 1950s and 1960s, a new civil-rights movement arose in the South. White-supremacist tactics were just as violent as they had been during Reconstruction. Blacks and civil-rights workers armed for self-defense.

John Salter, a professor at Tougaloo College and chief organizer of the NAACP's Jackson Movement during the early 1960s, wrote,

"No one knows what kind of massive racist retaliation would have been directed against grassroots black people had the black community not had a healthy measure of firearms within it."

Civil-rights professionals and the black community generally viewed nonviolence as a useful tactic for certain situations, not as a moral injunction to let oneself be murdered on a deserted road in the middle of the night. As the 1959 NAACP national convention resolved, "We do not deny but reaffirm the right of individual and collective self-defense against unlawful assaults." Dr. Martin Luther King Jr. agreed, supporting violence "exercised in self-defense," which he described "as moral and legal" in all societies; he noted that not even Gandhi condemned it.

The NRA Enters the Fray

National alcohol prohibition, enacted in 1920, spurred national violence, which resulted in the conservative Eastern business establishment – along with some religious pacifists –

demanding handgun prohibition. In their view, the solution to the failure of alcohol prohibition was more prohibition.

The handgun-prohibition campaign of the 1920s drew the National Rifle Association into the political arena, where it has remained ever since. The NRA had been founded by Union Army officers in 1871 to promote citizen marksmanship and civic virtue. Among its early presidents were Ulysses S. Grant (former president of the United States) and Winfield Scott Hancock("the hero of Gettysburg" and the 1880 Democratic presidential nominee).

In the 1920s, as today, the NRA's main political strength was its ability to mobilize its ever growing membership to contact government officials and express opposition to constricting the rights of law-abiding citizens.

After the NRA defeated the first handgun-prohibition campaigns, Franklin Roosevelt's first attorney general, Homer Cummings, attempted to push a bill to require the national registration of all handguns, coupled with a per-handgun tax that was more than a week's wages for a working man. Cummings hoped that his bill would set the stage for a handgun ban.

The handgun restrictions were part of the National Firearms Act (NFA), which also imposed stringent controls on machine guns and short-barreled shotguns. Once Congress heard from NRA members and removed handguns from the bill, the NRA dropped its opposition, and the NFA, including its severe controls on machine guns, became law.

Eighty-nine years later, the phony issue of "assault weapons" is based on a hoax invented by the gun-prohibition lobbies and spread by willfully ignorant media. There are some ordinary guns that *look* like machine guns. The Colt AR-15 rifle and the Ruger Mini-14 rifle are two examples. These guns do not function like machine guns. They fire only one round each time the trigger is pressed, just like any other ordinary gun. They are not more powerful than other guns; as rifles go, they are intermediate in power. That is why, in their most common caliber, .223, they are often used for hunting small game, such as rabbits or

> *The phony issue of "assault weapons" is based on a hoax invented by the gun-prohibition lobbies and spread by willfully ignorant media.*

coyotes, or midsize game, such as deer. In their most common calibers, they are not powerful enough for big game, such as elk or moose.

Yet many underinformed people think these guns are machine guns. They do not know that machine guns have been severely regulated since 1934. To acquire a machine gun requires a $200 transfer tax, fingerprinting, federal registration, and permission from local law enforcement. Since 1986, the manufacture of new machine guns for sale to anyone outside the government has been prohibited.

Gun-prohibition groups have fooled some people into believing that guns like the AR-15 are machine guns. As gun-prohibition strategist Josh Sugarmann explained in a 1988 memo, the guns' "menacing looks, coupled with the public's confusion over fully automatic machine guns versus semi-automatic assault weapons – anything that looks like a machine gun is assumed to be a machine gun – can only increase the chance of public support for restrictions on these weapons."

Today, semiautomatic handguns comprise 82% of new handguns manufactured in the U.S. Citizens buying such guns often choose guns with *standard* magazines holding 11 to 20 rounds. For rifles today, magazines of up to 30 rounds are factory standard.

Ordinary citizens choose these handguns, rifles, and magazines for the same reason that ordinary police officers usually do: because they are often the best choice for lawful defense of self and others.

Police officers who have a Springfield Armory semiauto pistol with a 16-round magazine on their hip and an AR-15 rifle with a 30-round magazine in their patrol car are not carrying those guns to go hunting or because they are intent on mass murder. These guns are standard police guns today because police, like ordinary citizens, know that criminals do not always attack one at a time and that violent attackers do not always fall down after a single hit – especially if the attackers are energized by methamphetamine or other drugs.

In such circumstances, the police officer, like the law-abiding citizen, may not have two seconds to spare to change magazines.

Tyranny and Genocide

Attorney General Cummings' repeated efforts for national gun registration were thwarted by the NRA. Then in 1941, Congress enacted the NRA's idea to ban gun registration.

Congress was looking in horror at mass shootings, and at mass murders by many other methods, taking place in Nazi-occupied Europe and in the Soviet Union. Congress could see how gun-registration lists compiled by democratic governments – such as the Weimar Republic in Germany or the Third Republic in France – were being used for gun confiscation once the totalitarians took over.

So when Congress passed the Property Requisition Act to allow the federal government to take property needed for national defense against tyranny, Congress made sure that the American people would retain their ability to resist tyranny. The 1941 act forbade the federal government to seize guns, to require the registration of guns (except for the guns already covered by the 1934 NFA), or "to impair or infringe in any manner the right of any individual to keep and bear arms. . . ."

Where Hitler or Stalin ruled, gun control was an essential step toward genocide. Gun-registration lists were used to confiscate guns from the prospective victims. After the victims were helpless, the extermination began.

Gun confiscation for genocide was not practiced solely by Hitler and Stalin. *Every* episode of genocide in the past century has been preceded by assiduous efforts to first disarm the victims: Turkish Armenia, the Holocaust, the USSR, Soviet-occupied Poland,

Guatemala under the military dictatorship in the 1950s, Mao's China, Chiang Kai-Shek's White Terror, Uganda under Idi Amin, Cambodia under Pol Pot, Srebrenica, Zimbabwe, Darfur. And many more.

Consider three steps: 1) registration; 2) confiscation; 3) extermination. Steps 1 and 2 do not always result in step 3. But step 3 is almost always preceded by steps 1 and 2.

Gun prohibitionists scoff at the idea that armed victims could fight genocide. History shows that they can. Especially in Eastern Poland, Belarus, and Lithuania during the Holocaust, some Jews were able to obtain arms and carry out guerilla warfare against the Nazis, saving many lives.

Of course not every government that uses registration lists for mass confiscation is intent on genocide. There is no genocide in Australia or Great Britain. But it is indisputable that the *genocidaires* seem to consider gun confiscation to be a crucial precondition for genocide.

* * *

During World War II and the early Cold War, gun control in America was not exactly a popular idea. As Americans were seeing, Nazis and Communists could inflict tyranny and murder because guns had previously been registered and confiscated.

Things changed in the mid-1960s. Violent crime was rising sharply. Race riots scorched nearly every big American city. The assassination of Martin Luther King Jr. in April 1968 and two months later of Senator Robert Kennedy (by a Palestinian angry at Kennedy's strong support for Israel) broke the dam.

In September, Congress enacted the Gun Control Act of 1968 (GCA). As amended, the GCA is the main federal law for ordinary firearms. Many state and local governments also enacted far-reaching new gun laws.

This was hardly enough to satisfy the prohibitionists. They aimed to do to the American people what the Ku Klux Klan had tried to do to the freedmen: disarmament, although this time, disarming people was said to be for their own good.

Their first major breakthrough was the District of Columbia in 1975. Acquisition of new handguns was outlawed. Use of any firearm for self-defense in the home was prohibited.

The most left-leaning state in America – Massachusetts – was supposed to be next, with a handgun-confiscation initiative on the ballot in November 1976. The gun-confiscation lobby called themselves People vs. Handguns. The people thought otherwise. Confiscation was rejected in a 69 percent landslide, partly because of widespread police opposition.

So prohibitionists decided that if they could not confiscate handguns, perhaps they could get the public to just ban new handguns. California's 1982 "handgun freeze" initiative was crushed, with 63 percent voting no.

The prohibitionists tried and failed again in 1993–94 in three left-leaning Wisconsin towns: Milwaukee, Kenosha, and Madison. The long-term result of the Wisconsin confiscation votes was that the people of Wisconsin voted overwhelmingly in 1998 (1,205,873 to 425,052) to add a right to arms to their state constitution.

Beginning with the first state constitution right-to-arms guarantee (Pennsylvania, 1776), 44 states now have a constitutional right to arms. In every state in which the people have had the opportunity to vote directly, they have endorsed the right to arms by landslide margins. Since 1968, the people of 23 states have chosen, either through their legislature or through a direct vote, to add a right to arms to their state constitution, to readopt the right to arms, or to strengthen an existing right. In addition, 37 state constitutions specifically protect the right of self-defense – sometimes as part of the arms right and sometimes stated separately.

Right to Carry

By the early 1970s, the legal carrying of handguns for protection in public places had been suppressed in most states. The typical system was that carrying required a permit; the permit required "good cause" in the view of a government administrator; and ordinary citizens who merely wanted to protect themselves were almost never considered to have good cause. About a half-dozen states were exceptions to this general rule.

Starting in Florida in 1987, state after state enacted licensing-reform laws. The laws prevented abuse of discretion by using objective standards. If an adult passes a fingerprint-based background check and a safety class, then she "shall" be issued a concealed-hand-gun carry permit. Today in 41 states, a law-abiding, competent adult has a clear path to a lawful concealed carry.

So in those 41 states, when Americans go to a shopping mall, a restaurant, a park, or most other public places, they are in a place where some people are lawfully carrying firearms.

Whether licensed carry causes a statistically significant decline in violent crime is a subject of scholarly debate. The evidence is overwhelming that there is no statistically significant *increase* in crime. In every state where "shall issue" has become the law, it has disappeared from the gun-control debate within a few years. Most Americans have acclimated to an environment in which public carrying of defensive handguns is common, safe, and unremarkable.

The right to keep and bear arms is not a 1791 anachronism. It is alive in the hearts and minds of the American people.

Forty-five years ago, it was common to assert that hunting was declining, so as a once-rural nation was now urban, gun ownership would soon be a discarded relic of America's past. However, the Second Amendment isn't just about hunting.

Rural, urban, and suburban, Americans have continued their 400-year-old practice of arming themselves more heavily than the people of any other nation in the world. As of 1948, Americans owned guns at a per capita rate about equal to what the French and Norwegians do now. (One gun per three persons.) Per capita gun ownership has tripled since then, so there are now slightly more American guns than there are Americans.

The right to keep and bear arms is not a 1791 anachronism. It is alive in the hearts and minds of the American people.

The Supreme Court

For a long time, the U.S. Supreme Court paid little attention to the Second Amendment, Likewise, the court was timid about the First Amendment for most of America's history; it was not until 1965 that it dared to hold that a congressional statute violated the First Amendment (*Lamont v. Postmaster General*, striking a statute requiring registration for exercising First Amendment rights).

Although the Second Amendment appeared in several dozen Supreme Court cases before 2008, it was almost always as a minor character – a typical individual right among a litany of other individual rights.

The court upheld the National Firearms Act (stringent laws about short shotguns and machine guns) in the 1939 case *U.S. v. Miller.* Unfortunately, the opinion written by the notoriously indolent Justice James Clark McReynolds was so terse and opaque that scholars spent decades arguing about what it meant.

The Supreme Court spoke up decisively in 2008. *District of Columbia v. Heller* ruled that the government could not ban the acquisition of handguns, nor could it ban armed self-defense in the home. *McDonald v. Chicago* (2010) ruled that state and local governments must obey the Second Amendment – just as they must obey the First Amendment and almost all the rest of the Bill of Rights.

THE PHILOSOPHY OF GUN BANS

Gun rights are not liberal *vs.* conservative, urban *vs.* rural, Democrat *vs.* Republican, or any other stereotype. The great Democratic Vice President Hubert H. Humphrey embodied liberalism's optimistic faith in the federal government and the federal Constitution. He believed that "one of the chief guarantees of freedom under any government, no matter how popular and respected, is the right of citizens to keep and bear arms. . . . The right of citizens to bear arms is just one more guarantee against arbitrary government, one more safeguard against the tyranny which now appears remote in America, but which historically has proved to be always possible."

In the culture war, the gun-prohibition movement has explicitly sought to make gun owners into social pariahs, like cigarette smokers: instead of being considered a personal right, gun ownership would be viewed as a repulsive personal habit. Dr. Mark Rosenberg, who in 1994 was director of the Centers for Disease Control's National Center for Injury Prevention and Control, stated that the CDC hoped to make the public perceive firearms as "dirty, deadly – and banned."

President Obama in January 2013 announced that he would be seeking more funds for CDC gun-control research. Much of this "research" has been junk science designed to create factoids about why ordinary people should not own guns. Even before 2013, the Obama administration was funneling grants to prohibitionists in order to produce antigun factoids as, supposedly, medical science. Guns are to be stigmatized as "disease vectors" and gun owners claimed to be disease carriers.

State-Imposed Pacifism

Gun prohibition has many bases, among them the pacifist-aggressives – people who want to use the force and violence of criminal law to make everyone else live by their personal philosophy of not using defensive force against violent attackers.

For example, the Presbyterian Church (USA) has declared that it disapproves of "the killing of anyone, anywhere, for any reason." Because the church believes defensive gun ownership is immoral, it supports the confiscation of all handguns. The United Methodist Church, which helped found the National

Coalition to Ban Handguns (now named the Coalition to Stop Gun Violence), declared that people should submit to rape and robbery rather than endanger the criminal's life by shooting him.

The Brady Center runs a "God Not Guns" coalition, which proclaims that the exercise of Second Amendment rights is inherently sinful, demonstrating a refusal to trust in God. Their work is promoted by Jim Wallis, an evangelical Christian who is the founder of the pacifist, hard-left *Sojourners* magazine and who is the leading figure of the Christian Religious Left in modern America.

Not all pacifist-aggressives are religious. Marxist and radical feminist Betty Friedan insisted that battered women must not use violence against their attackers because "lethal violence even in self-defense only engenders more violence." David Clarke, the father of the D.C. handgun and self-defense ban, claimed that his antigun laws "are designed to move this government toward civilization.... I don't intend to run the government around the moment of survival." In other words, it is more "civilized" for you to be murdered by a criminal than to defend yourself with a gun. A perverse definition of *civilization*.

For religious reasons or others, the gun-prohibition movement aims to outlaw self-defense with a firearm. As Sarah Brady announced to the *Tampa Tribune* in 1993, "To me, the only reason for guns in civilian hands is for sporting purposes." Her husband, Jim Brady, identified the circumstances in which he believes people should be allowed to possess handguns: "[F]or target shooting, that's okay. Get a license and go to the range. For defense of the home, that's why we have police departments." Sarah Brady's long-term goal, she told *The New York Times*, is a "needs-based licensing" system. Under the Brady system, all guns would be registered. The local police chief would decide if a person who wanted to buy a gun had a legitimate "need." Sarah Brady listed hunters and security guards as people who have a legitimate need, but not regular people who wanted guns for self-protection.

Gun prohibitionists denounce self-defense as a person's "taking the law into her own hands." This is false. Using deadly force or the threat thereof to defend against a violent felony is legal in all 50 states. There are many circumstances when exercising the choice to

Gun rights are not liberal vs. conservative, urban vs. rural, Democrat vs. Republican, or any other stereotype.

use force for self-defense or defense of another is entirely lawful. Using such force, therefore, cannot be "taking the law into one's hands" any more than exercising other lawful choices, such as signing a contract.

When criminals use force, though, they are violating the law and thereby taking the law into their own hands. When citizens use or threaten force to stop the lawbreaking, they are taking the law back from the criminals and restoring the law to its rightful owners: themselves.

The gun-prohibition movement is ultimately based on an authoritarian wish that the American people were not the people for whom the word *individualism* was coined by Alexis de Tocqueville. They yearn for America to be like Europe, where gun ownership is a sporting privilege for a few and not a right of the people.

They want a top-down society in which (supposedly) sophisticated and intelligent elites make wise and rational decisions about how ordinary people should live their lives. To these authoritarians, the self-sufficiency that gun ownership represents is an insult.

The authoritarians agree with the German sociologist Max Weber's 1919 lecture "Politics as a Vocation," in which he announced that the very definition of a state is "the monopoly of the legitimate use of physical force." Few

Americans have read Weber, but his principle has been the core of the gun-control movement and is anathema to the gun-rights movement.

Barack Obama

For whatever ideological reason, Barack Obama has a long record of embracing the antigun agenda. He is currently campaigning for a national gun-registration system. Instead of using the politically toxic word *registration*, he calls for a "national database" of guns. He endorses laws that he says will expand background checks. What he does not say is that every major congressional bill that has been introduced in the past several years under the title of "background checks" was written by Michael Bloomberg's staff and contained provisions for national gun registration.

Could prohibition then follow registration? Consider the record of Barack Obama before he became president. He endorsed handgun prohibition in general, and the D.C. and Chicago handgun-prohibition laws in particular. He endorsed the prohibition of all semiautomatic firearms (which are the overwhelming majority of new handguns and a large fraction of long guns).

He called for banning all gun stores within 5 miles of a school or park. This is the same as calling for a ban on gun sales, since every inhabited portion of the United States is within 5 miles of a school or park.

Ever since 1968, federal law has required that the only way a customer can purchase a firearm from a licensed retailer is through a transaction at the gun store, where the buyer picks up the gun. The only other place where the retailer may sell guns is at a gun show, and there the retailer must comply with all the same rules – such as background checks – as for sales for his storefront. (Hysterical claims about "Internet gun sales" ignore the fact that the Internet seller must ship the gun to a licensed firearms dealer in the customer's home state; the customer can only pick up the gun after the in-state dealer completes the standard background check.)

President Obama has endorsed legislation

to give the Bureau of Alcohol, Tobacco, Firearms, and Explosives nearly limitless discretion to outlaw rifle ammunition.

He proposed a 500 percent tax increase on guns and ammunition.

He has voted for legislation to ban every so-called assault weapon (very broadly defined) and even old-fashioned bird-hunting guns – such as every double-barrel and break-open shotguns in 28 gauge and larger.

Barack Obama has endorsed federal legislation that would eliminate the laws of the 41 states that allow ordinary citizens, after passing a fingerprint-based background check and a safety-training class, to obtain a permit to carry a concealed handgun for lawful self-defense.

WHO ARE THE SOVEREIGNS?

While some nations consider law to be the vehicle of the state, the American tradition views the law as the servant of the people. As a federal district court put it, "the people, not the government, possess the sovereignty" (*Mandel v. Mitchell*, 1971).

In the years leading up to the American Revolution, Patriots and Tories alike began to use the term "Body of the People" to mean "a majority of the people" and eventually "the united will of the people." Legitimate sovereignty, Patriots said, flowed not from "the Crown" but from the "Body of the People." Locating sovereignty in the people, and not in the Crown, meant locating the power to enforce the law in the people as well.

During the debate over ratification of the Constitution, federalist Noah Webster assured America:

Before a standing army can rule, the people must be disarmed, as they are in almost every kingdom in Europe. The supreme power in America cannot enforce unjust laws by the sword, because the whole body of the people are armed, and constitute a force superior to any band of regular troops that can be, on any pretense, raised in the United States.

It is true that the United States protects the right to bear arms more vigorously than other nations do. The U.S. protects most other rights better as well.

By reserving more power for themselves, Americans grant less power to the government. The American system of adversary courtroom procedure; jury trials; checks and balances among the three limited branches of government; the dual, limited sovereignty of local and national governments; and the widespread ownership of firearms all reflect the assumption that any government is not to be blindly trusted to control itself. Only if the people retain for themselves the direct right to enforce the law can the people's liberty be secure.

America chose to be different, a shining city on the hill, a beacon of freedom. From the very first days of colonial settlement, America rejected British and European precedent. That American laws recognize the right of individuals to use force for protection is consistent with the American principle of retaining extensive power in the hands of the people.

Simply put, Americans do not trust authority, as do the subjects of the British Commonwealth or Japan. Unlike the British, who so meekly acceded to their government's Firearms Act of 1920, they do not trust the police and government to protect them from crime. They do not trust the discretion and judgment of police officers to search whatever they please.

America places more faith in its citizens than do other nations. The first words of America's national existence, the Declaration of Independence, assert a natural right to overthrow a tyrant by force. In much of the world, the armed masses symbolize lawlessness; in America, the armed masses are the law.

George Orwell observed:

And though I have no doubt exceptions can be brought forward, I think the following rule would be found generally true: that ages in which the dominant weapon is expensive or difficult to make will tend to be ages of despotism, whereas when the dominant weapon is cheap and simple, the common people have a chance. Thus, for example, tanks, battleships and bombing planes are inherently tyrannical weapons, while rifles, muskets, long-bows and hand-grenades are inherently democratic weapons. A complex weapon makes the strong stronger, while a simple weapon — so long as there is no answer to it — gives claws to the weak.

Certainly the political ideology of the Founders of the American Republic and the authors of the Second Amendment was consistent with Orwell's viewpoint that dispersion of physical power in society is both a cause and an affirmation of dispersion of political power. Hubert Humphrey agreed.

One aspect of the American ideals of classlessness, individualism, and self-reliance is the archetypal hero. The armed Canadian hero is a government employee (the mounted policeman); the armed Japanese hero is an aristocrat (the samurai). Unlike the British knight (with expensive armor), the Japanese samurai (with a handcrafted, exquisite sword), or the Canadian mounted policeman (carrying a government-issued handgun that ordinary persons were not allowed to carry), the classic armed American hero – the cowboy – sported a mass-produced Colt .45 that could be bought at a hardware store.

The cowboy's Colt revolver was known as the great equalizer. The name is right because firearms make a smaller, less-powerful person functionally equal to a larger person. A firearm allows the smaller person to defend herself at a distance from the larger person. As an inscription on a Winchester rifle put it:

> *Be not afraid of any man,*
> *No matter what his size;*
> *When danger threatens, call on me*
> *And I will equalize.*

First Lady Eleanor Roosevelt lived this philosophy. As first lady and then as a civil-rights activist giving speeches in the segregated South, she spoke out for equality for all citizens. Because of death threats from the KKK and similar types, she carried a revolver for protection.

She was not a redneck, nor an angry white man, nor an insurrectionist, nor an enemy of the federal government, nor a conspiracy nut, nor any of the other things that antigun bigots claim about gun owners. She was a patriotic American and one of the world's greatest champions of human rights.

She led the U.S. delegation to the United Nations and helped create the Universal Declaration of Human Rights. Like the U.S. Declaration of Independence, the U.N. Declaration recognizes the necessity "as a last resort, to rebellion against tyranny and oppression."

The fundamental human right to keep and bear arms is the inherent right of all persons, not just Americans, to use firearms to protect themselves from large-scale criminals such as tyrants and *genocidaires* – and from lone criminals invading a home or attacking a school.

First American edition published in 2013 by Encounter Books,
an activity of Encounter for Culture and Education, Inc.,
a nonprofit, tax exempt corporation.
Encounter Books website address: www.encounterbooks.com

Manufactured in the United States and printed on
acid-free paper. The paper used in this publication meets
the minimum requirements of ANSI/NISO z39.48 1992
(R 1997) (*Permanence of Paper*).

FIRST AMERICAN EDITION

LIBRARY OF CONGRESS CATALOGING-IN-PUBLICATION DATA

Kopel, David B.
    The truth about gun control / David B. Kopel.
        pages cm. — (Encounter Broadsides)
    ISBN 978-1-59403-712-2 (pbk. : alk. paper)
    ISBN 978-1-59403-713-9 (ebook)
    1. Firearms—Law and legislation—United States—History.
    2. United States. Constitution. 2nd Amendment.
    3. Gun control—United States. 4. Sovereignty. I. Title.
            KF3941.K67 2013
            323.4'3—dc23
            2013004353

10 9 8 7 6 5 4 3 2 1